Journey of the WILDEBEESTS

BY BENJAMIN O. SAMUELSON

Gareth Stevens
PUBLISHING

Please visit our website, www.garethstevens.com. For a free color catalog of all our high-quality books, call toll free 1-800-542-2595 or fax 1-877-542-2596.

Cataloging-in-Publication Data

Names: Samuelson, Benjamin O.
Title: Journey of the wildebeests / Benjamin O. Samuelson.
Description: New York : Gareth Stevens Publishing, 2019. | Series: Massive animal migrations | Includes index.
Identifiers: ISBN 9781538216385 (pbk.) | ISBN 9781538216378 (library bound) | ISBN 9781538216392 (6 pack)
Subjects: LCSH: Gnus–Juvenile literature.
Classification: LCC QL737.U53 S26 2018 | DDC 599.64'59–dc23

First Edition

Published in 2019 by
Gareth Stevens Publishing
111 East 14th Street, Suite 349
New York, NY 10003

Designer: Katelyn E. Reynolds
Editor: Joan Stoltman

Photo credits: Cover, p. 1 Rob Reijnen/NiS/Minden Pictures/Getty Images; cover, pp. 1–24 (background) Vadim Georgiev/Shutterstock.com; cover, pp. 1–24 (background) CS Stock/Shutterstock.com; p. 5 GUDKOV ANDREY/Shutterstock.com; p. 7 Keertana Iyer/Shutterstock.com; p. 9 (map) Serban Bogdan/Shutterstock.com; p. 9 (wildebeest) Eric Isselee/Shutterstock.com; p. 11 Georgia Evans/Shutterstock.com; p. 13 Curioso/Shutterstock.com; p. 15 EcoPrint/Shutterstock.com; p. 17 Sergey Uryadnikov/Shutterstock.com; p. 19 JarrydH/Shutterstock.com.

Printed in the United States of America

CPSIA compliance information: Batch #CS18GS: For further information contact Gareth Stevens, New York, New York at 1-800-542-2595.

CONTENTS

WORDS IN THE GLOSSARY APPEAR IN **BOLD** TYPE THE FIRST TIME THEY ARE USED IN THE TEXT.

The World Cup OF WILDLIFE

The huge yearly journey, or migration, of wildebeests is known by many names. Some call it the "World's Greatest Wildlife **Spectacle**," others the "World Cup of Wildlife." It's even been called one of the "Seven Wonders of the Natural World." One thing's for sure: The wildebeest migration is one of the largest migrations on Earth!

Between 1.2 and 2 million wildebeests are moving throughout eastern Africa every day in a migration that never begins or ends. Plus, they've traveled this way for over a million years!

> ### THERE'S MORE!
> THERE ARE TWO SPECIES, OR KINDS, OF WILDEBEEST: THE BLACK WILDEBEEST AND THE BLUE, OR COMMON, WILDEBEEST. WILDEBEESTS ARE MAMMALS, WHICH MEANS THEY HAVE HAIR, BREATHE AIR, AND FEED MILK TO THEIR YOUNG.

Wildebeests are also called gnus (NYOOZ). They're in the same animal family as sheep and deer, even though they look a little like bulls.

5

Many Moving
MONTHLY

The wildebeest migration moves clockwise around eastern Africa, but no 2 years are ever the same. Wildebeests have no leader, instead traveling in megaherds. In a megaherd, smaller herds circle the main herd in different directions. The whole megaherd spins like a **tornado** as it moves in one main direction.

Wildebeest herds don't always move forward. They also go **backward** and to either side. They split up into smaller herds and gather to reform megaherds. They may walk in a long, solid line or spread out.

> ## THERE'S MORE!
>
> MEGAHERDS CAN TAKE 2 DAYS TO CROSS AN AREA! FEMALES AND THEIR YOUNG FORM HERDS OF 10 TO 1,000 ANIMALS WITHIN THE MEGAHERD. ADULT MALES TRAVEL ALONE. THERE ARE ALSO **BACHELOR** HERDS.

Wildebeest herds use swarm intelligence to move. This means each wildebeest decides what direction to move based on what its neighbors are doing. They **communicate** with each other to solve problems like where to find food and water.

7

Forever Finding FOOD

Wildebeests follow rains and the new grasses they bring. In fact, a rainstorm nearby can bring thousands of animals within a few hours! These herbivores, or plant eaters, eat continuously in the cooler morning and evening and rest during the hottest part of the day.

Because herds can eat up to 4,000 tons (3,600 mt) of grass in a single day, they're always on the move to find more grass. That's why herds have to spread out. One area doesn't have enough grass to feed everyone!

THERE'S MORE!

THE SERENGETI NATIONAL PARK IS ONE OF THE OLDEST AND MOST FAMOUS **ECOSYSTEMS** ON EARTH. EVERYWHERE WILDEBEESTS GO, INCLUDING THE SERENGETI, THEY **FERTILIZE** THE SOIL WITH THEIR POOP.

Wildebeests love to eat the short grass of the southern Serengeti National Park, but there's not enough grass or water to live there year round. After having their babies there, they leave as late as possible and return as soon as they can!

AFRICA

Serengeti National Park

TANZANIA

Indian Ocean

Bodies Built
FOR TRAVEL

Thankfully, wildebeests are built for travel. How else would they be able to migrate 6 miles (10 km) a day nearly every day of their life? Wildebeests cover long distances by **galloping** slowly for long periods. But if a predator is nearby, they can run 50 miles (80 km) an hour!

Perhaps one of the coolest—certainly one of the weirdest!—wildebeest features is the special flaps in their nose. These special pieces of skin act like doors, keeping dust out of wildebeests' noses!

> ## THERE'S MORE!
>
> ONE OF THE WAYS WILDEBEESTS COMMUNICATE IS THROUGH SOUND. THEY'RE OFTEN MAKING LOW, QUIET NOISES. IF THEY'RE BOTHERED, THEIR **SNORTS** CAN BE HEARD OVER A MILE AWAY!

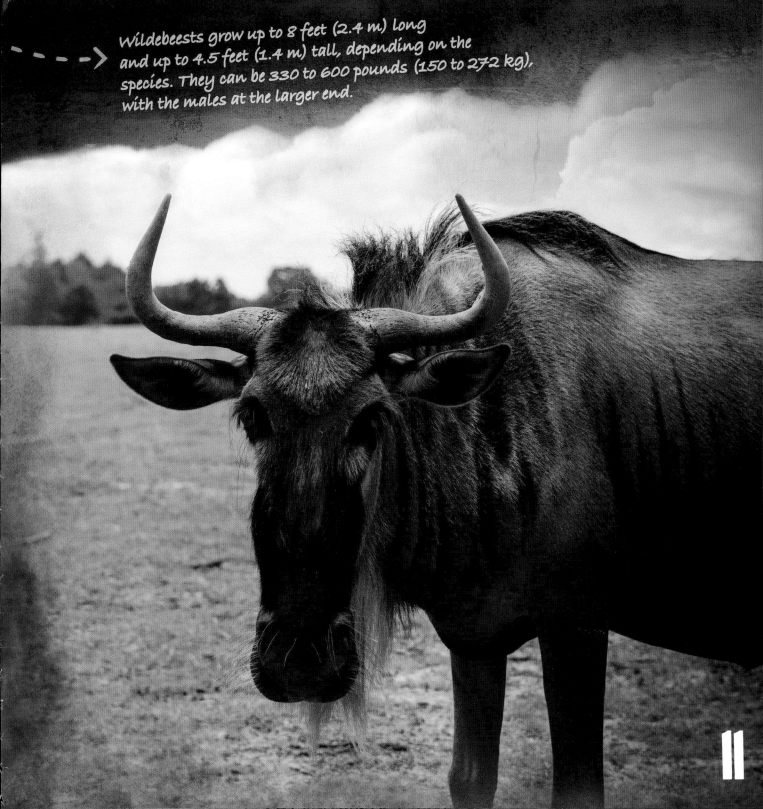

Wildebeests grow up to 8 feet (2.4 m) long and up to 4.5 feet (1.4 m) tall, depending on the species. They can be 330 to 600 pounds (150 to 272 kg), with the males at the larger end.

A Special Birthing GROUND

It's important that wildebeests give birth on the savanna, or grasslands, of the Serengeti. The Serengeti's short grasses have many **nutrients** that help females make very healthy milk to feed their young. Babies, called calves, quickly grow and fatten after birth so they can survive the migration.

Half a million wildebeests are born every year in the Serengeti. Calves are easy for hungry predators to catch. But if 8,000 are born a day, predators will get full quickly, and many calves will survive!

> ## THERE'S MORE!
>
> LIONS, CHEETAHS, AND OTHER PREDATORS EAT WELL DURING BIRTHING SEASON. IT'S IMPORTANT TO THE ECOSYSTEM THAT MANY WILDEBEESTS ARE BORN YEARLY. WITHOUT HIGH BIRTH RATES, THEY COULDN'T SURVIVE HAVING SO MANY PREDATORS!

Calves grow inside their mother for a long time. This gives them a better chance at surviving once they're born—and it works! Wildebeest calves can run 5 minutes after they're born!

13

The Clowns of the SAVANNA

In order to give birth to half a million babies every year, almost all female wildebeests **mate** every year! Then, a few months after giving birth, females choose mates again by deciding who **impresses** them.

Male wildebeests impress by galloping and bucking in a way that looks like dancing. They roll their heads and paws around in the dirt of their grassland homes to leave special smells for females. They won't stop to sleep or eat if a female is nearby! These actions have earned them the nickname "clowns of the savanna."

THERE'S MORE!

WHEN THE RUT, OR MATING PERIOD, ENDS, MALE WILDEBEESTS ARE REALLY TIRED! IT TAKES A LOT OF ENERGY TO SNORT, DANCE, AND FIGHT AROUND THE CLOCK.

Male wildebeests roll in pee and poop to tell other males to stay away from their area. But sometimes it doesn't work, and males fight. Scientists have found that male wildebeests have about 30 different fighting moves!

Surviving MIGRATION

The wildebeest migration crosses several rivers, including the Mara River and the Grumeti River. Not only are these rivers filled with hungry crocodiles, they're also very hard to cross. In 2007, the Mara River ran so fast after a huge rainstorm that 10,000 wildebeest died in a half an hour trying to cross it!

Usually, about 6,250 wildebeests die each year crossing rivers, giving crocodiles about 2 million pounds (900,000 kg) of meat to eat! As their bones break down in the water, nearby plants and fish get important nutrients they need to grow.

> **THERE'S MORE!**
>
> OVER 250,000 WILDEBEESTS DIE DURING EACH MIGRATION. SOME DIE OF THIRST, HUNGER, INJURY, OR TIREDNESS. OTHERS ARE HUNTED BY LAND PREDATORS, INCLUDING CHEETAHS AND LIONS.

A crocodile brings over half of its body out of the water while jumping to catch a wildebeest in its mouth. Then they bite down and pull the wildebeest into the water. It's quite a scene!

17

Surviving
PEOPLE

These days, wildebeests are running into many problems caused by people! Fences and roads have been built across their million-year-old migration paths. People have even cut down a quarter of the Mau Forest. This means the water coming down from the mountains normally held by the forest will dry up instead of feeding important rivers like the Mara.

Climate change has also affected Africa in a scary way. When rains stop, droughts occur. Food stops growing and many animals die.

THERE'S MORE!

FENCES CAN KILL. A FENCE BUILT IN BOTSWANA IN 1983 BLOCKED WILDEBEESTS FROM GETTING TO FOOD, QUICKLY KILLING 65,000. IN 1988, A FENCE IN THE CENTRAL KALAHARI BLOCKED WATER ACCESS, KILLING 50,000 WILDEBEESTS IN 4 MONTHS.

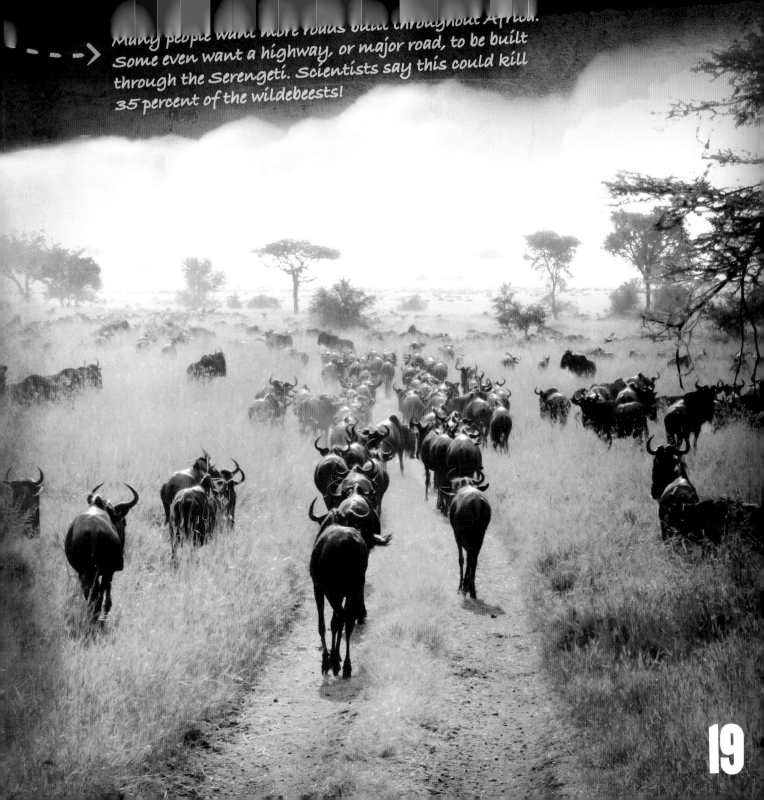

Many people want more roads built throughout Africa. Some even want a highway, or major road, to be built through the Serengeti. Scientists say this could kill 35 percent of the wildebeests!

A Keystone SPECIES

Wildebeests are a keystone species, which means every part of their ecosystem depends on them. They help make the soil rich with nutrients. They keep predators full so they don't have to eat other species, like giraffes. During migration, 300,000 zebras, over 12,000 **eland**, and at least 400,000 Thomson's gazelles even travel with them for safety.

Keeping wildebeests safe from fences, roads, and housing will need many different countries to work together. But it must be done because wildebeests are too important!

THE WILDEBEEST MIGRATION

Wildebeests travel between 1,000 and 1,800 miles (1,600 and 2,900 km) every year! At times, the herd moves in columns 25 miles (40 km) long!

DECEMBER–JANUARY
arrive in Serengeti

FEBRUARY–MARCH
birthing season

LATE MARCH
some begin moving north or west

APRIL–MAY
journey north begins for all, though some will move west before heading north

MAY
rut

JULY
journey continues north and northwest

AUGUST–OCTOBER
arrive at Mara River very thirsty; half the animals will cross the river, half will stay behind

NOVEMBER
begin heading south because there's no grass left

DECEMBER
following the rains, they continue south

21

GLOSSARY

bachelor: a young male animal without a mate

backward: opposite to the usual way

climate change: long-term change in Earth's weather patterns, caused partly by human activities such as burning oil and natural gas

communicate: to share ideas and feelings through sounds and motion

ecosystem: all the living things in an area

eland: a kind of deerlike animal that only lives on the plains of eastern and southern Africa

fertilize: to make soil richer and better able to support plant growth by adding something

gallop: to go at great speed

impress: to gain another's interest

mate: to come together to make babies. Also, one of two animals that come together to make babies.

nutrient: something a living thing needs to grow and stay alive

snort: to force air noisily through your nose

spectacle: something that draws attention because it is very unusual or very shocking

tornado: a storm in which powerful winds move around a central point

FOR MORE INFORMATION

Books

Bowman, Chris. *Wildebeests*. Minneapolis, MN: Bellwether Media, 2015.

Carney, Elizabeth. *Great Migrations: Whales, Wildebeests, Butterflies, Elephants, and Other Amazing Animals on the Move*. Washington, DC: National Geographic, 2010.

Shea, Mary Molly. *Wildebeests*. New York, NY: Gareth Stevens Publishing, 2011.

Websites

How the Wildebeest Migration Works
go2africa.com/africa-travel-blog/11704
Here you can read a month-by-month account of the migration and watch a cartoon that explains it.

Live Map of the Great Wildebeest Migration
discoverafrica.com/herdtracker/
See where the wildebeests are right now!

Wildebeest Migration Time-Lapse
blog.burrard-lucas.com/2014/10/wildlife-photographer-of-the-year-time-lapse/
This video takes 5 days of nonstop video recording of the migration and speeds it up to fit into less than a minute of video. It's amazing!

Publisher's note to educators and parents: Our editors have carefully reviewed these websites to ensure that they are suitable for students. Many websites change frequently, however, and we cannot guarantee that a site's future contents will continue to meet our high standards of quality and educational value. Be advised that students should be closely supervised whenever they access the Internet.

INDEX